Beading
BASICS
30 EMBELLISHING TECHNIQUES FOR QUILTERS

Mary Stori

PUBLISHING INC.

Love Note #4

by Mary Stori, 2001, 11 1/2" x 11 1/2"

DEDICATION

To the memory of my twin sister, Nancy Theobald Willmas (1946–2002). Her spirit will always shine like a thousand points of light!

ACKNOWLEDGMENTS

Once again, thank you, thank you, to two brilliant gemstones; my husband David and son Chris, and to our family's new treasure, Kelly Hayashi, for their love and support.

My heartfelt gratitude to each and every student for allowing me the opportunity to share my love of quilting and bead embellishment! In particular I wish to acknowledge: Helen Downie, Cindy Fitzpatrick, Francie Ginocchio (a.k.a. Spritzer Sister), Roz Grillo, and Jan Vander Hill for allowing their work to appear in this book.

Words of appreciation aren't sufficient for the crown jewels of editors: Darra Williamson, who made this book happen, and Cyndy Rymer, whose enthusiasm for the project was boundless. Congratulations to the dedicated staff at C&T Publishing for providing quality books and continuing the tradition of education and inspiration for quilters.

I'm indebted to Pfaff American Sales Corporation, Hobbs Bonded Fibers, Primrose Gradations, and Penny Taylor-Wallace of TWE/BEADS for their expertise and generosity.

Text © 2004 Mary Stori
Artwork © 2004 C&T Publishing

Publisher: Amy Marson
Editorial Director: Gailen Runge
Editor: Cyndy Lyle Rymer
Technical Editor: Karyn Culp
Copyeditor/Proofreader: Stacy Chamness
Cover Designer: Christina Jarumay
Book Designer: Staci Harpole, Cubic Design
Design Director: Diane Pedersen
Production Assistant: Jeffery Carrillo & Kirstie L. McCormick
Photography: Quilts by Sharon Risedorph and Kirstie L. McCormick unless otherwise noted; instructional photos by Diane Pedersen
Published by C&T Publishing, Inc., P.O. Box 1456, Lafayette, California, 94549

Front cover: *Meadow Flowers* by Mary Stori
Back cover: *Helen's Kimono* (page 20), *Love Note #4* (page 2), *Like Touching a Warm Cloud* (page 34), *Meadow Flowers* (page 1), and *Give Hugs*. Beading on the quilts listed by Mary Stori.

Attention Teachers: C&T Publishing, Inc. encourages you to use this book as a text for teaching. Contact us at 800-284-1114 or www.ctpub.com for more information about the C&T Teachers Program.

We take great care to ensure that the information included in this book is accurate and presented in good faith, but no warranty is provided nor results guaranteed. Having no control over the choices of materials or procedures used, neither the author nor C&T Publishing, Inc. shall have any liability to any person or entity with respect to any loss or damage caused directly or indirectly by the information contained in this book. For your convenience, we post an up-to-date listing of corrections on our web page (www. ctpub.com). If a correction is not already noted, please contact our customer service department at ctinfo@ctpub.com or at P.O. Box 1456, Lafayette, California, 94549.

Trademarked (™) and Registered Trademark (®) names are used throughout this book. Rather than use the symbols with every occurrence of a trademark and registered trademark name, we are using the names only in the editorial fashion and to the benefit of the owner, with no intention of infringement.

Stori, Mary.
  Beading basics : 30 embellishing techniques for quilters / Mary Stori.
    p. cm. Includes bibliographical references.
ISBN 1-57120-237-4 (paper trade)
1. Beadwork. 2. Quilting. I. Title.
  TT860.S77 2004
  746.46–dc22 2003028045

Printed in China
10 9 8 7 6 5 4 3

Table of Contents
WHAT'S INSIDE

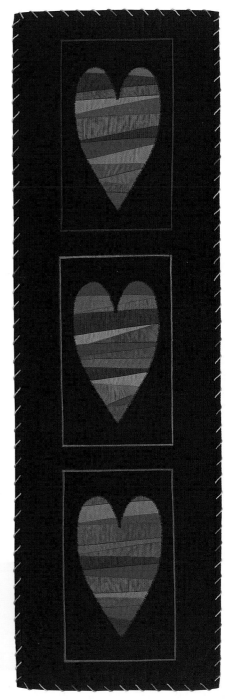

Love of Many Colors

by Mary Stori, 2002, 13" x 41"

Photo by Sharon Risedorph

A former cooking school owner, I now embellish fabric with beads, instead of garnishing food. What began as a mere flirtation, has become a true passion. I see a quilt and it screams "Bead me!" I love the look and feel of beads, and I don't have to do the dishes after my "play time" is over. The process of beading stimulates my mind, and provides an extraordinary sense of contentment. Now if I could just figure out a way to bead while soaking in a bubble bath, sipping a glass of champagne...ahhhhh!

I'm hopelessly in love with the challenge and look of bead embellishment, yet my ideas are sometimes ten steps ahead of my current skill level. Therefore, hundreds of hours have been spent perfecting the craft of attaching beads to fabric, resulting in fun new techniques to share. Don't let this scare you. I've spent the time experimenting so you don't have to! I always assure my students that "I don't do hard." What I do might be a little time-consuming, but never difficult. Beading allows the fun of quiltmaking to continue when (not if) I choose. Always remember, you are in charge of the needle and thread! You are supposed to be having fun, so fall in love with quilting all over again as you explore my unique approach.

Interest in bead embellishment has reached all skill levels of quilters, from beginners to accomplished stitchers. Along with this newfound curiosity comes a need to learn the proper methods to attach beads to fabric surfaces. Beads adapt to a diversity of sewing styles for both traditional and contemporary artists. Ample evidence is provided throughout these pages. You'll discover a variety of construction methods and styles, such as: traditional machine piecing, foundation piecing, hand or machine appliqué, hand embroidery, and hand or machine quilting. Incorporating the pizzazz of beads is sure to keep you engrossed during the process, no matter which construction method you prefer.

Quiltmaking offers a wonderful opportunity to express yourself. Don't be afraid to color outside the lines; create quilts that shine brightly from your heart, and, of course, from beads!

Mary Stori

Ice Storm

by Mary Stori, 2002, 22" x 27"

This winter scene is the first in a series depicting the four seasons of a white oak tree on our property. The tree branches were embellished by stacking seed beads into clusters, while the appearance of ice crystals and snow was created by Scatter-stitching seed beads onto the background fabric.

Hello, and welcome to a front-row seat in my beading class. This visual guide to beading on fabric surfaces will be like having your own private instructor; the location and time is up to you. It offers a solid foundation to create bead accents on quilts, garments, and other decorative items with simple, clear, hands-on instructions. You'll learn fundamental stitches to attach beads, charms, buttons, and other trinkets to your projects. Once the basics are understood, you'll happily discover that most techniques are simply combinations or variations of the basic stitches. Sagging beads and untidy threads on embellishments will be gone forever!

A discussion of materials and equipment needs will acquaint you with this new medium, and helps avoid unnecessary expenses. Because very little equipment is required other than beads, and no beading experience is necessary, you'll be able to begin stitching with beads almost immediately. Embellished quilts are usually created as wallhangings, and should hang square and flat. Garments should drape nicely on the body. To assure success, guidelines offering various stabilizing are provided.

Recently, much of my time has been concentrated on developing the perfect final touch: beaded quilt bindings. Once you recognize the fabulous impact these techniques achieve, the bindings of your existing wallhangings will tempt you. And don't overlook the possibilities of incorporating these ideas to garments or household items. My methods include beadwork that mimics lace, resembles pyramids, texturized dots and dashes, diagonal strings, netting, and organic trim. Readers who are familiar with my bead embellishment techniques will be delighted to investigate this new direction.

Use this book as a guide to develop your expertise and confidence as you learn to bead onto fabric. To use it as a reference book, consider adding a spiral binding. Any large office-supply store can add a spiral binding, or do a three-hole punch, for a minimal fee.

Finally, and I say this in total reverence, technology has sent men to the moon, yet no sewing machine has been developed that can substitute the hand-sewn beadwork techniques presented in this book. That's perfectly okay with me because I don't think of myself as a sprinter, rather a marathon runner. I'm simply enjoying the journey! Whether you are a beginner or an experienced quilter, garment maker, or craft hobbyist, you'll find these techniques will ensure your embellishments will be skillfully and creatively applied, presenting your projects with a new eye-catching dimension!

Tropical Nine-Patch

by Francie Ginocchio, 1999, 30" x 30"
Photo by Sharon Risedorph

The Basic Bead Backstitch was used with pony and seed beads on and around the hand appliquéd vines and leaves to represent drops of water. The quilt was created for a Bali™ fabric challenge. It was machine quilted with variegated Sulky rayon thread.

Lighting Your Way
BEFORE YOU BEGIN

When traveling down a new path, it's helpful to have brightly illuminated street signs to help you find your way. Please get acquainted with the following introductory information. Starting off with the appropriate supplies and properly prepared fabric will light your way, adding to your beading enjoyment.

Bead Styles and Sizes

Beginners may get dizzy reviewing all the options available. You'll be relieved to know that most of the beading techniques in this book offer complete flexibility and adaptability to countless types and sizes of beads. Unlike beaders who create a woven necklace by following a charted pattern, specific bead sizing is usually not a big concern for this category of beadwork. My rule of thumb is simple: if a green bead can become a grass skirt, why then, it's perfect!

If you are new to this medium, the following brief introduction to bead types will help you, so read on. Beads are categorized by shape, size, and finish. Additionally, you'll find variations in the quality and size specifications between manufacturers. Trade names for almost identical types of beads differ from one manufacturer to another; this can add to your confusion. Locating a knowledgeable supplier, and good record keeping on your part, is the best way to avoid repeating costly mistakes.

Hawaiian Moo-Moo

by Mary Stori, 2001, 33" x 36"
Photo by Sharon Risedorph

This play on words was inspired by one of my quilting tours to Hawaii. Numerous beading techniques are featured, such as bead strings for the grass skirt, bead appliquéd fern palm tree and silk flower leis, Washer/Nut coconuts in tree, bead embroidery details, as well as buttons, charms, and trinkets.

Good Morning
by Mary Stori, 2002, 24" x 24"

Designed as a workshop project for students on one of my Hawaiian quilting tours, this quilt was assembled entirely with bead appliqué. Beading techniques such as Washer/Nut, Scatter-stitching, Picot, and Lace all contribute to the whimsy of the design.

Bead importers/distributors sell beads by weight, usually not less than one kilo (1 Kilo = 2.2 pounds) per type/color of bead. (Which is a heck of a lot of beads!) You can purchase smaller amounts of beads at a variety of retail stores such as craft, hobby, independent bead shops, chain fabric stores, vendor's at conferences/shows, mail order, and via the internet (see Resources, page 48). These retailers most often sell beads that have been repackaged into tubes, containers, plastic bags, individually, by bulk weight, and by the "hank." Hanks of beads are merely strings of beads gathered into one unit. The cost, the number of strings per hank, and the number of beads on each string will vary according to the type of bead. Buying repackaged beads is a good way to obtain a large variety of beads, but when the project calls for lots of beads, it's more economical to get beads by the hank.

NOT SUCH A BARGAIN

Purchasing "bargain" bags of beads may not turn out to be a bargain if the beads are poor quality. It's not unusual to find that they are misshapen, contain rough or jagged edges, are inconsistently sized, and/or the color is poor. Beading is time consuming; don't add to it with unnecessary sorting or return trips to the store to get beads that you can actually use. Keep good records, noting where the beads come from and at what price. I record all of my purchases; my memory can't be trusted.

After spending one day in a workshop with me, students tell me that they go home to paw through their costume jewelry and take it apart to access beads. Treasures found at garage sales and thrift stores can also be a wonderful, inexpensive source of interesting beads.

Storage

Beads need to be stored so they are accessible. To prevent damage, avoid keeping your supply in a damp area, or one that is exposed to high heat (like near a heating vent). The best advice I can share is to place your stash in a convenient location. If you can't get at your beads, you won't use them! Inexpensive plastic storage containers with dividers or drawers are ideal. These items can be found at sewing stores in the notion section, or even the hardware department at your nearest discount store. Recycled containers such as empty bead tubes or small boxes, spice jars, small baby food bottles, or film canisters are good choices. To easily identify the contents, hot glue a bead to the lid. Resealable plastic snack or sandwich bags are handy to store larger quantities of beads.

A Bead by Any Other Name

A brief description of the most common types of beads available are listed and pictured on page 9.

SEED BEADS

As a general rule, seed beads are small and resemble a seed, thus the name. These nearly round beads are available in a number of sizes, ranging from size 16° (the smallest) to size 6° (the largest).

Similar to the numbering system of our sewing needles, the larger the size number, the smaller the seed bead will be.

It's interesting to note that seed beads manufactured in the Czech Republic are fairly circular, often irregularly shaped, presenting a "bagel-like" profile. Japanese seed beads however, are a little more square, more uniform in size, and will have slightly larger holes. Incidentally, most bead shops carry and sell size 11° seed beads, the size I use most often because of the vast choices of colors and finishes available, and their reliable performance for these techniques.

DELICA BEADS

At first glance these Japanese-manufactured specialty beads are mistaken for seed beads. On closer examination, the difference is apparent. A Delica bead looks more like a short tube with thin walls. It's favored by beaders when a consistent size bead is required, and for its larger and more uniform hole, ideal when passing thread through the bead several times. The flat ends allow the beads to sit snugly together when stitching straight lines, which gives a nice uniform look.

SIZE 6° SEED BEADS

As the size number indicates, these are larger size seed beads. They are getting special attention in this section because I use them a great deal when beading bindings. The choices of colors and finishes are numerous.

Spinning Pinwheels

by Roz Grillo,
30" x 30", 2003,
beaded by Mary Stori
Photo by Sharon Risedorph

The placement of the directional Scatter-stitched bugle beads, and their reflective quality, contributes to the spinning effect of the pinwheels.

SIZE 5° TRIANGLES

This specialty bead is also manufactured in Japan. As the name implies, the shape is triangular and slightly larger than a size 6° seed bead. The bead colors are often described as "color-lined." Some beads are clear with a colored lining, others are colored beads, such as green with an orange lining. This bead style also decorates many of my bindings.

2-CUT BEADS

These beads, which are made in the Czech Republic, and can be difficult to find, are usually available at bead shops. The shape appears to be half bugle bead (tube like) and half seed bead because it's often small and has polished ends. They are similar to a 3-Cut bead, but not as faceted.

3-CUT BEADS

The name of these beads refers to the manufacturing process of passing glass canes through a grinding machine three times to achieve a raw-chopped effect to the bead. Like any faceted surface, the light-reflective properties add a lot of sparkle.

BUGLE BEADS

These glass "tubes" are available in a number of sizes. Just to keep us on our toes, the numbering system is not consistent with seed beads.

Unlike seed beads, bugle beads are sized differently: the smaller the bead size number, the smaller the bead.

The smallest is a size 2°; the most common is size 3° (about ¼" long). I have a special fondness for a variety called twisted bugles. The "twist" of the lining color gives a spiral appearance to the glass bead, which adds great sophistication and sparkle. Interestingly, they are smooth inside and out!

Bugle beads: size 2°, 5°, and 3°

Size 11° Silver-lined green seed bead (Czech Republic)

Size 11° red seed bead (Japan)

Size 11° Delica gold seed bead (Japan)

Size 8° black seed bead

Size 6° red seed bead

3-cut blue iris

2-cut green iris

Size 5° topaz iris triangle

Be Kind to Your Beads

This may come as a big surprise to you. The gorgeous blue glass bead that has caught your attention may not be blue glass. Instead, the lining of the glass bead may have been painted or dyed. Why should you care?

The color of glass beads, and even the coating of some metallic beads, can be altered as a result of laundering, dry cleaning, the heat and moisture of a steam iron, and even from ultraviolet rays from the sun.

Perhaps you don't plan to expose your work to any of these conditions, yet it's still a darn good idea to check for colorfastness (of any type of bead) before you begin a project. It's easy to do.

TIP

To test for colorfastness, drop a few beads into a small container of warm, sudsy water and shake a bit. Allow them to rest for an hour or two before draining. After they've dried, compare them to the unwashed beads to determine whether the appearance has changed. Further test the beads by placing some beads on a windowsill that receives direct sunlight. After a few days, check the condition against the original beads.

Silver-lined beads are a personal favorite of mine due to the richness of color. Unfortunately, these beads can tarnish over time. It's most noticeable on clear or silver beads that turn dark. Avoid laundering your beaded projects; they are fragile and may not survive the trip through the washing machine. Instead, to remove dust, vacuum them using a clean brush attachment on the hose. Or you might consider laying a clean screen mesh over the quilt and lightly vacuuming with the hose nozzle. If a piece requires more cleaning, hand wash and remove as much water as possible by rolling it between towels, then laying it flat to dry. Before dry cleaning any bead-embellished piece, check with your dry cleaner to be sure they are experienced.

Here's a tip I share when teaching workshops; stitch a few beads inside a cuff, pocket, or hem of a garment—no need to mention it to your dry cleaner—then examine and compare them for changes after they've been cleaned.

Basic Supplies and Equipment

Here's the good news. You probably already own all or most of the following basic supplies. Refer to Resources, page 48, to locate sources.

NEEDLES

A short, thin, strong needle will be suitable to use for the majority of the techniques presented. My preference is a Jean S. Lyle Quilting Betweens, size #10. The eye of the needle is large enough to thread easily, yet it passes through the fabric and most beads smoothly. Because some stitches require traveling through the bead/bead string more than once, a slightly longer, thin needle, such as an appliqué, Sharp, or Straw needle, (size #11 or #12) will be useful to have on hand. I don't use beading needles because even though they are very thin, they are too long, bend too easily, and they're not worth the hassle when stitching through fabric layers.

NYMO BEADING THREAD

This super strong nylon thread is available in various thicknesses. I use size D, a good medium-weight thread that is very suitable for sewing through fabric, yet can pass through most size 11° seed beads more than once. Sewing through fabric can

wear the thread; a worn thread is a weak thread. I prefer to work with a single 16"–20" length of thread. In the unlikely event the thread breaks, replacing fifty beads is less daunting than a thousand. Making a diagonal cut at either thread end can help in the threading process. To avoid unnecessary tangles or knots, run your fingers snugly along the length of the thread (before or after threading onto the needle) to relax the kinks. I haven't found it necessary to wax or condition this thread to bead quilts or garments.

Another rule of thumb is to match the color of the thread to the bead, or use a neutral color such as gray or beige. However, if there is high contrast between the color of the fabric and the thread, consider changing the thread color to match the fabric instead. Nymo is available in a range of colors. There are some techniques that allow the thread to be somewhat visible; therefore, careful consideration when selecting your color will be beneficial.

SCISSORS

Very sharp embroidery scissors that cut at the tip, or a small sharp thread snip is essential for trimming thread close to the fabric, and to obtain a crisp diagonal end cut.

BEADING FRAME

Whenever possible, bead with your fabric secured in a hand-held PVC frame to maintain proper tension and eliminate puckering and distortion. The integrity of the fabric's grain can be comprised when fabric is placed in a round quilting or embroidery hoop because it will stretch in every direction. This is not advisable. Instead, use an 11" x 11" or 11" x 17" PVC-type lap frame. I recommend this frame because these shapes and sizes are very comfortable to use, the edge of the frame does less damage to the fabric, and the tension is far easier to control.

Here's a trick I use when it isn't possible to attach the clips to the frame without damaging previously beaded sections: Wrap the excess fabric over the outside edge and slightly underneath the frame. To achieve adequate tension, secure the layers in place by basting with white thread, or use small safety or straight pins.

MISCELLANEOUS HINTS

Use a good, bright light to reduce eyestrain and improve accuracy in beading. Your stitches will only be as good as your vision. Bring your frame along with you the next time you get your eyes tested. Your vision specialist can adjust your glasses as necessary.

Ready, Set, Bead

I like to work sitting on our comfortable denim couch, with my feet up on a coffee table, my beading project and beading supplies on a lapboard to steady everything. However, when working with a large variety of beads, I'll exchange the lapboard with a large jellyroll baking pan. If the beads spill, they fall into the pan, not on the carpet. Naturally, sitting at a table to work is more conventional, but because I live life to the fullest (and come from a weak gene pool) it's not as comfortable for me due to my bad back. Numerous containers, dishes, or specialty bead trays can be used to hold the beads as you sew. Miniature muffin tins, paint palette trays, shallow dishes, or even ashtrays can be utilized. Avoid soft plastic materials that can dull the needle as you gather up the beads. When using a small number of beads, scatter them on a piece of leather, rough side up. You'll find the beads are easier to pick up when they don't skitter around.

PREPARATION

A little preplanning leads to a successful outcome, but it's not necessary to have a grand plan. Some of my "how come I didn't realize this would happen?" experiences have led to success because it forced me to take an "off-ramp." By leaving the comfort of the familiar, I've had to improvise and develop techniques/solutions that would never have occurred to me otherwise. I'm encouraging you to experiment! Use these techniques as instructed; then try altering the bead size, shape, and color. New combinations are just waiting to be discovered.

Before committing fully to the project, test-stitch one or more techniques using several types and colors of beads to judge the impact. Analyze the appropriateness of the bead selection to your fabrics. For instance, if your goal is drama, be sure the color and sparkle of the bead doesn't get swallowed up by the print of the fabric! Likewise, if the desired

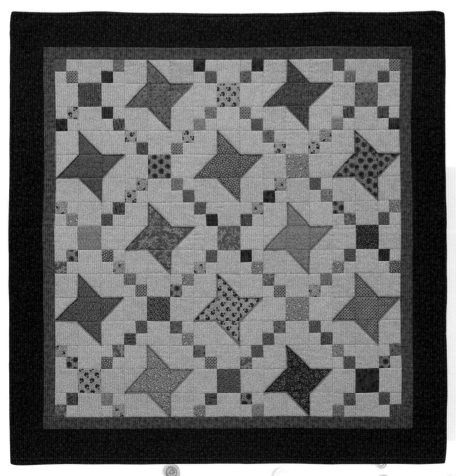

Civil War Stars

by Jan Vander Hill, 2003, 56" x 56"
Beaded by Mary Stori
Photo by Sharon Risedorph

Crazy Chain pattern published in *Scrap Frenzy*, by Sally Schneider, Woodinville, WA, Martingale & Co., 2001

The Picot Edging Method (see page 39) was used to outline the patchwork stars. The antique matte finish of the brass seed beads contributes texture and a sense of strength.

mood is subtle, scattering small beads might be more effective than beading bugle beads in a row.

The importance of stabilizing new work will be discussed in a minute. You are not limited to beading just your own creations. Household items such as pillows, table linens, lamp shades, and, of course, clothing can be canvases for beadwork.

Try to hide the thread path and knots to achieve a tidy appearance. For instance, when incorporating beads onto a lined garment, stitch from the right side, hiding all knots under the bead whenever possible. Bead through the top layer (fashion fabric) and pass the thread (unseen) between its lining.

When stitching through very heavy fabrics, consider using a double strand of thread for extra support.

Use a removable marking tool if reference marks are necessary. You'll love my fail-safe method of using soap slivers—yes, good old-fashioned hand soap. Avoid brands that contain cold cream because they tend to crumble. Chill a bar of soap in the refrigerator. Once the soap is cold, shape one side using a vegetable peeler or emery board for a narrow edge. Reshape the edge as necessary. A damp (not soaking wet) dishcloth will remove any markings still visible after beading without damaging the beads or fabric. Mark as you go, as the soap has a tendency to rub off quickly.

Stabilizing Guidelines

One of the major reasons beaded quilts do not hang flat and square on the wall, and why bead-embellished garments don't drape properly on the body, is because the fabrics were not adequately stabilized. Quilters understand that the quilting process can cause uneven shrinkage and puckering to their work. Beading can have that same effect if steps aren't taken to control it. For instance, when beading a single motif with a high concentration of beads in one area, you are likely to develop distortion in the surrounding fabric. Avoid this problem by stabilizing the fabric prior to beading. If a minimal amount of small beads are evenly distributed throughout a project, stabilizing may not be necessary.

With years of experience behind me, I've created some basic guidelines that you can apply as needed. Please be aware that these are simply guidelines, not rules. Projects can differ greatly in regard to construction methods (hand vs. machine), design style (pieced vs. appliqué), sub-styles (hand appliquéd or fused), and quilting technique (hand vs. machine). All of these particulars will impact "if, how, and when" to stabilize. Your preferred method of working will be the biggest guiding factor; it's usually best to begin with a few decisions. For example, if machine quilting is the only type of quilting you do, note the pros and cons offered below and plan accordingly. This list applies to quilts, though some methods translate equally well to garments.

STABILIZE WITH BATTING

This is the method I use most often. After preparation of the quilt top (any construction method), thread baste (or safety pin if you must), a layer of batting to the wrong side. My batting choice is Hobb's Thermore® for small projects, Hobb's Heirloom Premium® or Fairfield's Cotton Classic® for larger pieces (see Resources on page 48). These two layers are now treated as one, and because batting is a necessary addition, it makes sense to use it as the stabilizer. Additionally, the beading thread will be hidden between the layers once the backing is added.

STABILIZE WITH MUSLIN

Quilts that feature a scenic hand-appliquéd background and foreground can be stabilized by stitching the designs onto a muslin foundation, followed by beading. If you plan to hand quilt the piece when the appliqué is complete, cut away the muslin wherever possible to avoid stitching through excess layers. For machine quilters it's not necessary to remove the muslin layer; just stitch carefully around the beads.

STABILIZE WITH FUSIBLE PRODUCTS

I use two distinctly different types of fusible products to stabilize fabric for beading. The first is a lightweight paper-backed adhesive web used to fuse two layers of fabric together when preparing machine appliqué designs. It will support a high concentration of beading while remaining pucker-free, yet passing the needle through the extra layers is only slightly more difficult.

Fusible tricot interfacing is a good choice to stabilize lightweight opaque fabrics, such as silk or rayon, that will be used in garment construction. The prepared fabric will remain quite drapable with the ability to accept a fair amount of beadwork without fabric distortion.

Quilting Techniques: Pros and Cons

How and when to quilt will probably have the biggest impact on your stabilizing decision. The advantage of machine quilting is the ability to easily stitch through many layers, which will expand your stabilizing options greatly. The hand quilter's choices are more limited because the thickness of the cloth layers must be minimized. When you quilt after you bead, the hand quilter can easily maneuver around beads, whereas the beads can interfere with the movement of the pressure foot when machine quilting. Even with free-motion quilting (without a pressure foot) the possibility of damaging the beads or the fabric still exists. Your expertise at the machine, combined with the amount of quilting and beading, will all contribute to your success.

BEAD BEFORE QUILTING

I prefer to bead the stabilized quilt top prior to quilting whenever possible, so the thread and knots will be hidden in the quilt sandwich. When using this approach it's important to understand that the thread tension of the beadwork to the fabric is established, and it should remain constant. Be aware that the shrinkage that occurs in both hand and machine quilting can have adverse effects on the way beads lie on the work, which is especially noticeable when bead designs are stitched one after another in lines or concentrated patterns.

Hand quilting will generally cause less distortion. If machine quilting is your preference, reduce the amount of quilting and sew just enough to hold the layers together. Excessive quilting, when precision beading is featured, will ruin the appearance of the bead motifs.

If the quilt's design focus is the beadwork, the quilting is not the first feature you should notice.

QUILT FIRST, BEAD LATER

Consider quilting first. The beads can then be added by stitching through all three quilted layers. However, if you prefer to avoid visible threads on the backing, catch the top two layers only when beading. It may not be possible to stabilize the work in a frame and obtain enough play in the fabric for this latter approach. To avoid fabric distortion pay special attention to the thread tension as you bead.

QUILT AND BEAD AS YOU GO

Here's a third idea that translates well when machine quilting is desired. It's rather unconventional, but provides lots of flexibility during the construction process. Keep in mind this method is limited to quilts no larger than about 30" x 30" because the quilting doesn't penetrate all three layers. Here's the thought process and procedure I used for *Meadow Flowers* (on the title page).

After the quilt top was pieced I decided that the quilting design should appear in the background. This meant the stitching had to be done before any other elements were added. A layer of batting was basted to the wrong side of the top to stabilize it, then the spider web motif was quilted through these two layers.

For well-formed stitches, and to allow the quilt to travel over the feed dogs without catching, place a piece of blank newsprint (or freezer paper, do not press to fabric) underneath the batting and remove it after quilting.

The next step in *Meadow Flowers* was to fuse the stems and leaves in place. Then I added texture to those areas with machine stitching. The buttons and beads were attached by sewing through the two quilted (stabilized) layers. Finally, the quilt backing was added and secured only by stitching in the ditch between the patchwork border and the center rectangle. The scant amount of quilting holds the layers together sufficiently to compensate for the weight of the beads, but has no harmful affect to the bead designs. If the project doesn't have borders, I skip stitching through all three layers entirely. It's no problem as long as the quilt top remains small and isn't embellished with rocks!

The ABC's
OF BEADING TECHNIQUES

The best way to learn the following methods is to follow the step-by-step exercises. I urge you to grab a needle and thread. You can create a bead sampler and gain confidence as you stitch along with me.

Evening Workout Video: Take 2
by Mary Stori, 1996, 22" x 22"

Holstein cows are a favorite subject of mine and this cutie was created for "Character Traits," a traveling exhibit of art quilts from the Midwest. I was assigned the letter "C." A galaxy of random Scatter-stitched star sequins were created using the Washer/Nut Method to highlight the night sky.

BASIC BEAD STITCHES

Although there are many approaches, I'll concentrate on my favorites for attaching beads to cloth. There are two categories of techniques in this book, the Basics that form the foundation of beading, and Beyond Basics, which are variations on elementary beading techniques translated into decorative motifs.

I've developed a distinctly different approach to the position of the work during the stitching process. My lack of formal training allowed me to create unorthodox ways to achieve the accuracy I desired, while developing a more comfortable approach to sewing. The instructions reflect my personal preference of stitching toward myself, from top to bottom. It is easier to create most stitches if you bead vertically, which makes it just plain easier to place the needle precisely. I also experience less hand/wrist strain because my wrist isn't held in a tightly twisted angle as it was when sewing along a horizontal plane. To acquaint you with this new stitching direction, picture your beading frame as a clock, with the top being 12 o' clock and the bottom as 6 o' clock.

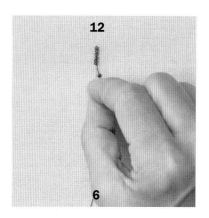

Notice how the line of vision is improved when stitching from top to bottom.

Note: Black thread was used in all of the photos to make the examples clearer.

United We Stand

by Mary Stori, 2002, 44" x 29"

The glitter of the 4th of July sparklers was created by Scatter-stitching various types and colors of beads along a sewn line.

There are probably other names for this knot, but so many quilters use it, they've claimed it as their own. This variation makes a slightly larger knot that guarantees it won't work its way through the weave of the fabric.

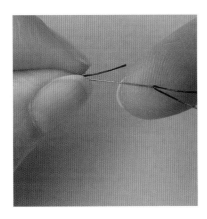

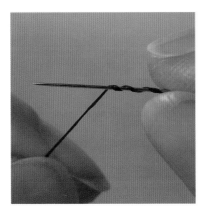

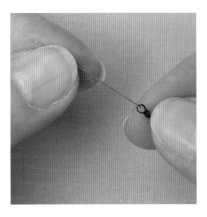

1. Thread the needle with a 16" length of thread. Hold the needle horizontally by the eye using the forefinger and thumb of one hand. Use the other hand to position the cut end of the thread toward the eye of the needle.

2. Hold the cut end with the finger and thumb near the eye of the needle. Wrap the thread tightly around the needle 6 times. Think of this as a French knot that is laying down.

3. Keep the thread taut and rotate the needle to a somewhat vertical position. Pinch the wrapped thread loose enough to travel over the eye of the needle, but tight enough to prevent it from unwinding. Tug downward to move and then trap the knot between the forefinger and thumb. Use your free hand to pull the tip of the needle, and allow the thread to slide over the eye of the needle and down to the end, where the knot will form. Clip the tail to about $^1/_8$".

Heartfelt

by Mary Stori, 2001, 11 $^1/_2$" x 11 $^1/_2$"

Dense wool or felt adapt beautifully to bead applique, without the need of turning the edges under! Here contrasting and matching color seed beads are scatter-stitched following the outline of the motif. They perform as design elements as well as contributions to the construction process.

LOCK STITCH

Use this stitch every time you start a new thread. The Lock stitch helps to take the strain off the thread and prevents the knot from popping through the fabric. It is not a substitute for the tie-off knot used to end the thread.

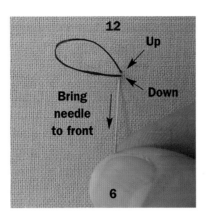

1. Thread the needle and knot one end with a $1/8$" tail. Enter the fabric from the wrong side, where the first bead will be placed, and pull the thread completely through to the right side. Insert the needle through the fabric to the wrong side, about 3 threads of the weave below where the thread came to the right side (toward 6 o' clock).
2. Next bring the needle to the right side about 3 threads below where the thread passed to the wrong side (again, at the 6 o' clock side).

TIE-OFF KNOT

When the beading is done prior to sandwiching the quilt, this knot is executed beneath the fabric, directly under a bead. The weight of a heavy bead can pull it forward, allowing excess thread to remain in the space between the bottom of the bead and the fabric. To avoid this problem, firmly push the bead onto the quilt top while you take a tiny backstitch into the wrong side of the fabric. Once the bead is secured, finish with a tie-off knot. When the beading takes place after the quilt is completed, make (and hide) the knot beneath the bead, on the right side of the fabric. You'll need about 5" of thread to make the knot.

The wrapping motion will always be: under (when you enter the loop), over (the thread loop), and back under (the thread loop).

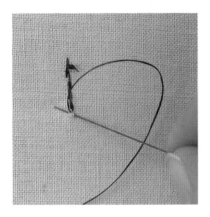

1. Take a tiny stitch into the fabric, very near the point where your thread exited, under the bead.

2. Pull the thread almost, but not all the way through, leaving a loop. With your needle, enter the loop from underneath.

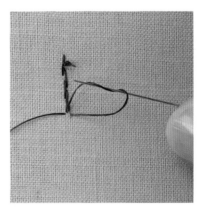

3. Use the needle to travel over the thread and back under. Pull the thread firmly so the knot rests tightly against the fabric. Clip, leaving a $1/8$" tail.

Instead of trying to skewer a seed bead onto your needle, try "popping" it on.

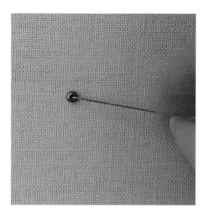

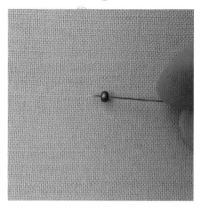

1. Lay the needle on top of the seed bead, with the tip positioned to sit over the center of the hole.

2. By exerting slight downward pressure on the needle, the bead will pop right onto the tip!

SINGLE-BEAD BACKSTITCH

I prefer this Basic Bead Backstitch to stitch a single bead, a straight or curved lines of beads, or for scattering beads onto fabric. I am rewarded with consistent results and durable stitching for any type of bead. Each bead is locked snugly in place and the thread tension is automatically maintained. Once you learn this simple technique, and some modifications, you'll know how to execute about **50%** of the techniques I use.

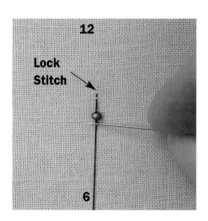

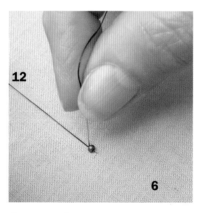

TIP

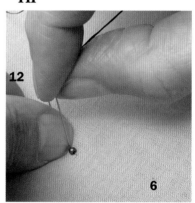

1. Begin with the Lock Stitch (described on page 17), then pop a bead on your needle and let it slide down the thread to the fabric.

2. Enter the fabric, 1 bead width from where the thread came up, toward the 12 o' clock side of the frame. Pass the needle and thread completely through to the wrong side. Congratulations! You've made your first stitch!

To achieve accurate spacing, draw the thread tightly toward the 12 o' clock side of the frame. The bead will roll over the Lock Stitch, positioning the hole parallel to the fabric. Use the thumbnail of your other hand to hold the bead in place, and enter the fabric between the bead and your fingernail.

This technique is simply a continuation of the Single-Bead Backstitch, used along a line you've marked, a motif printed on fabric, or to outline patchwork or appliqué.

NOTE: For faster results, you may wish to use the Bead Embroidery Method (see page 26) when the bead design is very compact.

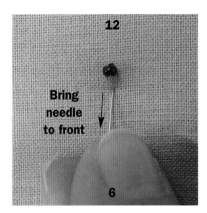

1. With one bead in position and the threaded needle on the wrong side of the fabric, bring the needle to the right side one bead width from the **6 o' clock** side of the bead you have just stitched, pulling it completely through.

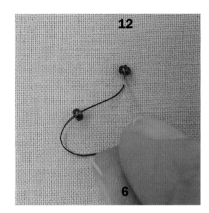

2. Thread another bead onto the needle and reinsert the needle close to and directly in line with the previous bead. (The **6 o' clock** side of the first bead.) Take care not to pierce the thread. Repeat until the desired length has been reached, pass the needle to the wrong side of the fabric and tie off.

Love Note #2

The Single-Bead Backstitch method is a good choice to use when precise lines are desired. This lettering is an example.

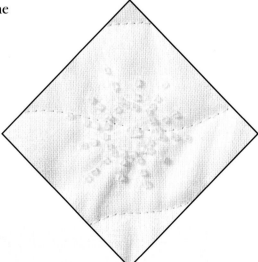

Nali

by Mary Stori, 2002, 16" x 16"

Short, straight-line beading adds sparkle to this snowflake print fabric. To reduce the sharpness or definition of a line, leave small spaces by stitching slightly more than one bead distance between beads.

To achieve well-aligned and better-defined results, use the Single-Bead Backstitch (see page 18) on intricate and detailed designs. This stitch is not any more time-consuming than ripping out badly spaced beads sewn 5 to a stitch (see Bead Embroidery Method on page 26), and the stitching is more secure. Because the beading path is a curve, you may find your perspective of "one bead width" a little off. Experience will conquer that problem quickly.

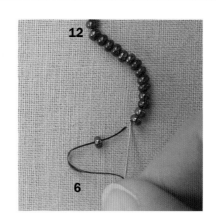

Using the Single-Bead Back-stitch, note that the change of direction to accommodate the curve is always made when the needle passes up from the wrong side. In the photo the needle came back up at about the 8 o' clock position. String another bead and re-enter the background fabric by aiming for the thread of the previous bead, without piercing it.

Helen's Kimono

by Helen Downie, 2003
beaded by Mary Stori
21" x 21"

Subtle beading decorates this traditionally machine-pieced patchwork Kimono quilt. Well-defined curves and circles, sewn using tiny Delica beads and a single Curve-line Backstitch, highlight the fabric's design. (The pattern was published in The Changing Seasons, by Jill Liddell, Dutton Studio, 1992, printed by permission of designer and quiltmaker.)

We can all use more time, right? This technique will speed up the beading process and is especially helpful when the project is large. Follow the directions for curve-line beading, but this time add one bugle bead after each seed bead. A size 3° bugle bead can cover the space of at least 5 size 11° seed beads! Spacing along a curve is slightly more challenging because of the bugles' longer length, so until your skills improve consider positioning a bugle bead onto the work as your guide.

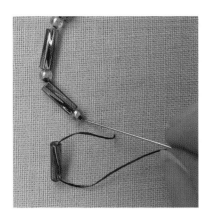

Variation 1: Stitch by alternating 1 seed bead and 1 bugle bead. Aim for the thread of the previous bead, but don't pierce it. Re-enter the background fabric about 1 thread of the weave of the fabric below the previous bead.

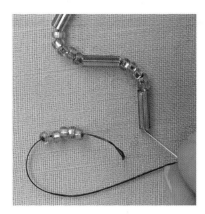

Variation 2: Use seed beads as spacer beads for sewing tighter curves. Stitch several seed beads, in one stitch, for spaces that might be too tight for a bugle bead. When the curve becomes more gentle, begin alternating bugle beads and seed beads.

In The Pink

by Mary Stori, 1997
14" x 20"

Here's an example of quick curve-line beading along a gentle curve. Alternating seed and bugle beads makes the stitching go more quickly and distinguishes the flower's stem and leaves from the rose which was stitched using the seed bead curve-line method.

This multi-function technique helps overcome irregularities from inconsistent bead sizes or improper spacing by straightening any continuous length of beading. Many beginners have trouble getting a stitched line of beads to lie flat. This usually means that not enough space was left for a bead to sit, therefore it "jumps" out of line. On the other hand, if too much space is allowed, the background fabric and the beading thread may be visible and distracting. Both of these problems can be overcome by straightening the line of beads using this technique.

For projects that may be subjected to more wear, such as a garment, this method provides additional strength. Before executing this technique for the purpose of straightening, strengthening, or for a duel purpose, complete your line of beading, tying off as usual. Begin again by threading a fine appliqué needle with a new length of thread. Make it longer than the distance of beads to be straightened or strengthened.

1. Bring the needle up from the wrong side, just underneath the last bead, and pull the thread completely through to the right side. **2.** Enter the "tunnel" of beads, traveling as far as possible. Exit by pulling the thread completely through the beads and re-enter the next bead in the line. Do not take a stitch into the fabric. The thread must travel the entire length of the beads with one continuous thread until the end of the line. Pull the thread firmly to adjust the line smoothly and pass the needle to the wrong side and tie off.

Child's Play

by Mary Stori, 2002, 36" x 36"
Photo by Sharon Risedorph

The eye-catching beaded binding echoes the primitive feeling of the hand embroidery designs, while adding a little pizzazz to this simple, homespun patchwork quilt. (See page 46 for beaded binding instructions.)

ZIGZAG SCATTER STITCH

For subtle glints of light, rather than continuous-beaded lines, distribute or scatter beads over the fabric. The actual stitch is very similar to the Single-Bead Backstitch (page 18). It differs because the beads are stitched approximately 1"–1 1/2" apart. To create the appearance of random placement, the sewing order resembles a zigzag and is worked in vertical "rows," filling in blank spaces as the following "row" is stitched. For proper thread tension, always pull the thread completely through before taking the next stitch. You'll enjoy the speed of developing this extra dimension to your work!

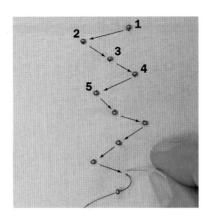

1. Attach one bead using the Single-Bead Backstitch, coming up about 1" away below and to the left of the first bead. **2.** Add a 2nd bead, coming up about 1" away, below and to the right of this bead. **3.** Add the 3rd bead, come up below and again a little to the right. **4.** After the adding the 4th bead, change directions by coming up below and to the left, and add the 5th bead. **5.** Continue adding beads in this manner, sewing in a diagonal direction, alternating the direction about every 3 beads.

Evening Workout Video: Take 2

Scatter-stitching secures star sequins to enhance the feeling of a night sky. (See Washer/Nut method on page 25.)

DIRECTIONAL SCATTER STITCH

This version of the Single-Bead Backstitch can add visual movement and will direct the eye to specific areas of interest. The distance between the beads can vary to accommodate the purpose of the beadwork, but it's a good idea to keep the spaces less than 1 1/2" apart. Execute the stitch as directed on page 18, following a stitched line and leaving spaces between each bead. Vary the bead type, color, and distance according to your needs.

United We Stand

The glitter of the 4th of July sparklers was created by scatter-stitching various types and colors of beads along a sewn line.

This is a quick way to fill specific areas. Its uses are similar to the hand embroidery Satin stitch. When filling in a design (as shown at right), begin in the center and work to one side, then finish filling in the other side. Use the backstitch as you bead to help maintain better thread tension. Since the beads don't sit as securely to the fabric with this technique, the line of beads will appear slightly elevated. In addition to filling in small motifs, this versatile stitch can also be used to create many patterns, such as radiating lines around a center bead or button, brickwalk, meandering pathways, and fans.

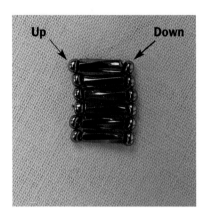

A seed bead, bugle bead, and a seed bead are treated and stitched as 1 unit. Rows of identical bead units can quickly form pathways, fans, or other design elements.

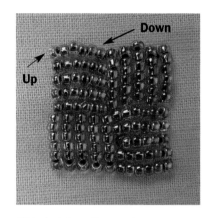

This brickwalk pattern was created by stitching 5 rows of 6 beads each, first horizontally (upper-left corner), then altering and adding 5 more rows vertically (lower-left corner).

1. Bring the threaded needle up from the wrong side at the point the line will begin. (Begin in the center if filling in a design; work to one side first, and finish by filling in the other side.)

2. String on numerous beads and pass the needle straight down through the fabric at the end of the last bead you strung.

3. Come up at least one bead's width from the previous row at the point where the first row began.

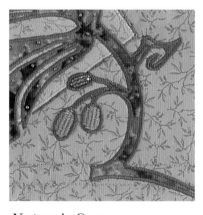

Nature's Own
by Cindy Fitzpatrick
beaded by Mary Stori

The "berries" were beaded using the Lazy stitch to fill in the areas within the satin stitched outline. See fullview on page 32.

Now that you know about 50% of the techniques I use, you can add another 20% with this very flexible technique. It's easy to understand the mechanics of the stitch if you think of it in hardware terms. (My husband is retired, so hardware terminology is common.) Use it to hold a bead or other object in place with another bead; this also helps to hide the thread. The embellishment item you wish to feature will be the "Washer." The "Nut" is a smaller bead that holds the Washer down. Be sure the Nut is larger than the hole of the Washer. The thread acts as the "Bolt" securely fastening the Washer and Nut to the fabric.

Washers will help add interest and personality to your projects. Use large seed beads, various types of beads such as bulge beads, pearls, or triangles, sequins, charms, sea shells, plastic trinkets, and buttons; just about anything with at least one hole can be added. Heck, if an object doesn't have a hole, just add one with a small drill. You aren't limited to one featured item. Try stacking three or four seed beads to create texture; note the layer of ice in *Ice Storm* in the photo to the right.

Always begin this technique with a Lock stitch. Embellishments can be sewn individually and tied off after each one. Smaller details easily translate to Scatter stitching (see page 23).

Ice Storm

Seed beads are stacked to create a layer of ice on each branch. See quilt on page 4.

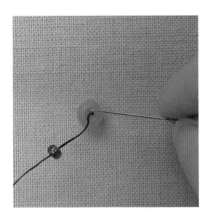

1. Bring the threaded needle up from the wrong side where the embellishment is to be placed, and then string on one large bead (Washer), allowing it to slide down the thread to the fabric surface. **2.** Add a smaller bead (larger than the hole of the Washer), pass the needle back through the hole of the large bead and through to the wrong side, bypassing the smaller bead.

All of these items have been attached using the Washer/Nut Method.

Like Touching a Warm Cloud

The mylar discs, which represent bubbles, are attached with a clear seed bead.

BEYOND BASICS

Many of the following decorative techniques are simply variations of the basic stitches you've already explored. Other techniques teach you some new approaches, and all are fun and guaranteed to enhance your projects with texture, complexity, and winks of color. Consider working with slightly longer thread for these methods to avoid constant tying-off. You'll probably find that an appliqué needle works best when stringing and passing back through multiple beads.

BEAD EMBROIDERY METHOD

The term *bead embroidery* generally refers to beading on cloth, or reproducing thread embroidery stitches with beads. It's a variation of the Backstitch, in which 5 beads (or any other number) are strung and stitched as one unit. They are anchored by backstitching through the last 1 or 2 beads.

Many bead artists consider it the standard method of attaching beads to cloth for compact, intricately beaded designs. I avoid using this method to embellish quilts for 3 reasons. The first is that only 1 or 2 of the 5 beads are firmly secured (backstitched) to the fabric. Those beads now contain 2 strands of thread, which may make it difficult to straighten or strengthen the line. It's also tedious to precisely bring the needle up from the wrong side between the line of beads without piercing the original thread. This, of course, is a purely personal opinion; you may find it an effective method to bead more quickly.

However, use this stitch when you are beading sheer or very lightweight fabrics because it's less stressful to the cloth.

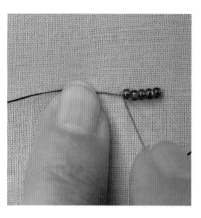

Bead Embroidery Stitch
1. Work horizontally. Bring the threaded needle to the right side of the fabric. String 5 beads and let them fall down the thread to the fabric so they lay in a line. Use the tip of the needle to position the beads to sit snugly in line by pushing back on the last bead strung as you re-enter the fabric at the very end of that bead.

2. Bring the needle back to the right side, within the line of beads, between the 3rd and 4th bead strung, taking care not to nick the thread. Pass the needle through the hole of the last two beads strung (#4 & #5) and repeat this process.

Here's a great way to have fun experimenting by translating your favorite embroidery stitches into bead designs.

1. Begin with a Lock stitch, bringing the threaded needle to the right side of the fabric where you wish to place the motif. String 12 seed beads onto the thread and, working clockwise, pass the needle back through the 1st bead strung.

2. For better visibility and maneuverability when sewing, reposition the string of beads to lay in a counterclockwise position. Now add 1 size 6° seed bead and pass the needle (clockwise) through the 6th bead strung. Pull the thread gently, yet snugly, to allow the larger bead to flip to the center to form a flower head.

3. Anchor the design by reinserting the needle into the background fabric, working out all the excess thread, and finish with a tie-off knot on the wrong side of the fabric.

Hawaiian Moo Moo

This Hawaiian Bovine beauty is wearing a floral lei created with several daisy stitches.

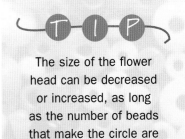

TIP

The size of the flower head can be decreased or increased, as long as the number of beads that make the circle are sufficient to surround the center bead.

Couching is a method of attaching items to fabric with stitches that travel over the detail to be secured. I don't recommend this method for attaching a string of beads. The results aren't as strong as the Single-Bead Backstitch. Use it as a decorative technique, for example, to attach braid by couching with short strings of beads. In addition, consider using this technique when the Washer/Nut Method (see page 25) isn't sufficient to secure the embellishment.

Bring the thread up to the right side, close to the braid. String a sufficient number of seed beads to completely cover the thread as it crosses over the braid, to the point where the needle re-enters the background fabric. Pass the needle completely through and repeat as necessary.

ARCH

To create an arch, string an uneven number of beads onto the thread, take the stitch into the fabric by one or more beads less than the distance spanned by the beads. Because the space is reduced, the beads pop up to form an arch. The height of the arch can be made greater or smaller by adding or subtracting the number of beads on the string (but always use an uneven number) and/or changing the length of the stitch. This decorative stitch is so adaptable. Try varying the length of the stitch, and the number, type, and combination of bead styles for unexpected results.

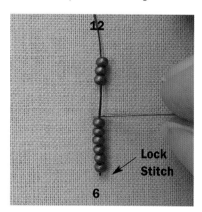

12

Lock
Stitch

6

Begin with a Lock stitch and pass the needle to the right side of the fabric where the arch will be positioned. String 9 seed beads onto the thread. Reinsert the needle through the fabric, between the 6th and 7th bead, to shorten the length of the stitch and allow the beads to form an arch.

Meadow Flowers

Small bronze and gold beads were used to create tiny garden spiders using the Arch method.

Good Morning

To add dimension, the rooster's tail feathers are color splashed with arches of red bugle beads. The stitch length was shortened by about the length of one bugle bead.

Here's a three-dimensional shape to enhance your next project, a simple yet decorative touch that can be incorporated into many quilt or clothing styles.

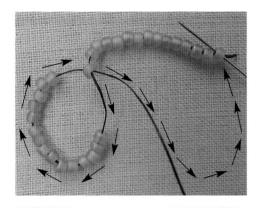

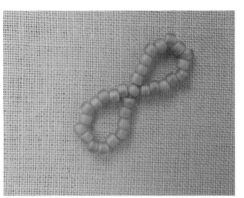

Begin with a Lock Stitch and pass the needle to the right side. String 30 seed beads and pass the needle through the 15th bead strung, in the same direction the originally strung. Pull gently to form a circle on the lower half of the string. Now pass the needle through the first bead strung, again as originally strung.

When the thread is pulled a circle is formed, creating a bow tie.

Here's another easy motif to add texture. Alter the appearance of this technique by varying the sizes and colors of the beads. Similar to the Arch Method, the space of the stitch is reduced, when the thread is tightened the beads form an upright triangle unit.

Make a Lock stitch and pass the needle to the fabric's right side. Thread 3 size 11° seed beads and 3 size 2° bugle beads alternating sizes. Pass the needle through the first bead threaded, and into the fabric as close to where the thread began as possible, without hitting it. Pull completely through to the wrong side and tie off.

Meadow Flowers
Individual triangle units, consisting of bugle beads, size 2°, and size 11° seed beads, were stitched consecutively around the button to represent flower petals.

This technique is a longer version of the Washer/Nut Method (see page 25), in which the last bead strung (often a seed bead) becomes the Nut that locks the line of beads together. When multiple units of dangles are stitched along the border or edge of a project, they are usually referred to as fringe. You'll never tire of experimenting with the number, size, style, or color of beads and other embellishments!

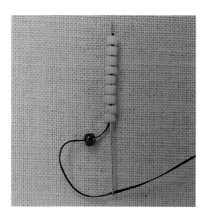

1. After completing the Lock stitch, pass the needle to the right side of the fabric. String on as many beads as you wish the length of the fringe to measure. **2.** Skipping the last bead strung, pass the needle back through all of the beads in the string, and into the fabric, exiting on the wrong side. If it becomes difficult to travel back up the string it's usually because you've pierced the original thread. You will need to remove the needle and begin again. Pull the thread completely and tightly through the string. You'll lose a little of the tightness when you tie off.

Hawaiian Moo Moo

Three dangles grow out of the center of a size 6° seed bead that provides a base to support their weight. To add interest, each dangle was stitched using a different combination of beads.

Note: This is also an example of the Bead Appliqué Method (see page 33).

DANGLES WITH ACCENTS

It's easy to incorporate charms, decorative beads, and other embellishments using the principles of the basic dangle. The featured item will hang from the center of a loop of beads at the end of the bead string. Again, the variations are only limited to your imagination!

1. Start with a Lock stitch, emerging on the right side of the fabric at the point where you want the string of beads to begin. String 9 seed beads, size 11°, add 5 seed beads, size 11°, add the charm or decorative item, and another 5 seed beads, size 11°. **2.** Pass the needle back through the first 9 beads strung, reinserting it into the fabric right next to the spot where it first emerged, and adjust the thread tension. Be careful as you pass back through the beads so the thread is not split or weakened. Finish with a tie-off knot.

In this example, the loop holding the heart is barely visible because the beads are the same color.

This version of a dangle can work as a single string (dangle) or in a row as a fringe edging. The goal is not necessarily to create identical units; it's more interesting to allow the "branches" to grow out of the central string wherever you please.

1. Make a Lock stitch, then bring the needle to the right side of the fabric. String 15 seed beads, size 11°, and bypassing the last bead strung, re-enter the main trunk, passing the needle up through 4 beads, exiting between the 10th and 11th beads strung. Pull the thread completely through.

2. Now string about 4 more beads, and bypassing the last bead strung, pass the needle through the 3 beads of this branch and re-enter the central string at the point where this branch began. Travel back up a few more beads, exiting where you want the next branch to be. You'll need to adjust the thread tension as the branches grow. Continue moving up the main string until you reach the top, passing the thread to the wrong side and tie off.

Meadow Flowers
A branched fringe unit was stitched through 1 buttonhole, while the other hole contains 2 units of varying length.

Fuller fringe units can be achieved by adding sub-branches to each branch as they "grow."

The striking appearance of this technique belies its ease of stitching. Each bugle bead is interlocked to the previous bead by weaving the thread through the bead as the stitches are made. This is what enables them to stand upright. This technique can be worked either in a vertical or horizontal direction.

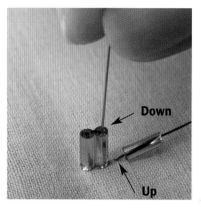

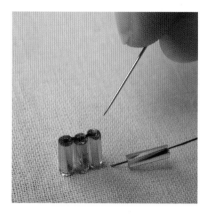

1. Begin with a Lock stitch, passing the thread to the right side of the fabric where the wall is to start. String 2 bugle beads onto the thread and allow them to slide down to the fabric. Use your fingers to stand them upright, side by side. Re-enter the fabric directly beneath where the second bead will sit, passing the needle to the wrong side. Note: In this example, the stitch was worked from left to right.

2. Bring the needle back to the right side, just beside the second bead. String a 3rd bugle bead onto the thread and pass the needle back through the second bead through the second bead to the wrong side.

3. Again, bring the needle to the right side, this time next to the 3rd bead. Add another bead and continue as described, always locking the current bead you are adding in place by going back through the previous bead.

LONG BUGLE BEAD WALL

Another variation can be applied to "walls" that measures at least 6" or longer. Once the wall is stitched, lay a section flat on the fabric and take a tiny stitch between 2 of the bugle beads, crossing over the thread, and repeat to provide ample strength. Bend another section of the wall in the opposite direction and take 2 more tacking stitches, and continue as desired.

Nature's Own

by Cindy Fitzpatrick, 2003,
31" x 36"
Photo by Sharon Risedorph

A twisted bugle-bead wall decorates a portion of the machine appliquéd flower.

It doesn't get much better than this: appliquéing and embellishing at the same time. Items that are best suited for bead appliqué have finished edges, such as: ribbons, trims, laces, and silk flowers. Fabrics that won't unravel when cut like Ultrasuede™, dense wools, felt, and layers of fabric fused together are other good choices. Many of the Basic and Beyond Basic beading techniques presented in this chapter can be used as an appliqué stitch. The examples provided below should help fire up your imagination.

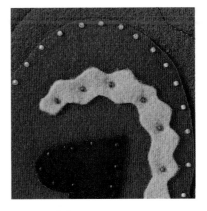

Heartfelt

Dense wool or felt adapt beautifully to bead applique, without the need of turning the edges under! Here contrasting and matching color seed beads are scatter-stitched following the outline of the motif. They perform as design elements as well as contributions to the construction process.

Summertime

by Mary Stori, 2003
22" x 27"

The small silk leaves are bead appliquéd to the quilt using the Single-Bead Backstitch method. Rather than tying off after each leaf, the thread traveled between the quilt layers before coming up again to add another leaf.

The Bright Side

BEADED BINDINGS

And you thought your quilts were finished? Not yet; let the fun continue! I predict this to be the newest trend in bead embellishment.

The idea of adding beads to the outside edges of my quilts came about quite by accident. After completing a Christmas tree wall quilt, I found the impact of the central theme was exactly as planned. Yet, by the time the eye traveled to the outer edge, the charm of the design fell flat. By adding beads along the seam line of the binding to represent an evergreen swag, dotted with red berries, the components became integrated and the overall effect was incredible. I refer to these moments as "design opportunities."

Gosh, that was so rewarding I began testing other ideas. Once I recognized the fabulous effect my experiments achieved, the bindings of my existing quilts began to tempt me. These bead accents can provide a gentle frame or a highly dramatic influence to all styles of quilts.

To enhance the spirit and individuality of each quilt, its design and fabric selection can be coordinated with suitable bead styles, colors, and edging techniques. Recognize too, that many of these

Like Touching a Warm Cloud

by Mary Stori, 2002, 17" x 19"

The title and inspiration for this quilt came from a comment made by Nancy Garver of Oberlin, OH, as she described a mohair shawl on display at Liberty of London during one of my quilting tours. The Mylar "bubbles" are attached using the Washer/Nut method. The pearls in the tub were stitched with the Single-Bead Backstitch, and the lacy binding treatment continues the "ahhhh" feeling of the quilt.

GETTING READY TO BEAD A BINDING

techniques can be utilized on areas other than bindings. Consider duplicating one of these methods on purchased ribbon or trim and apply it as a decorative border or edging on curtains, tablecloths, napkins, bed linens, or pillows.

Before you let loose your sense of style, review the following general tutorial before practicing the edging treatments. Next, grab your beads and begin "finishing" your quilts or other projects.

Binding

Bind your quilts using a continuous, double-fold, straight-grain (not bias) binding strip to assure adequate stability. Mitered corners work best.

Thread

In general, work with a single long length (25"-30") of Nymo, size D. If the design constitutes several rows of netting or mesh made up of bugle beads, you may want the security of using doubled thread. The flexibility of the mesh, in conjunction with the often sharp ends of bugle beads, increases the risk of damage to the thread.

Needles

Use a quilting Between when stitching individual beads, and the longer appliqué (Sharp or Straw) needle when adding multiple beads.

Beads

Experiment using a variety of bead types; keep in mind that the final design should not overpower the quilt's design. Some of my favorites are small seed beads, size 10° or 11°; 3-Cuts; and bugle beads, size 2° or size 3° (plain or twisted). They all work well independently or when joined to create a pattern. Triangles and larger seed beads, size 6°, produce effective binding accents when attached with small seed beads. The size and shape of the bead of course will contribute to the overall impact, but color can make or break the design too. Sometimes (sadly, as none of us have any extra time to waste), the appropriateness or the "what was I

thinking" factor is only apparent after numerous inches have already been beaded. Chalk that up to a character building moment and try another approach.

When reproducing some of these techniques, you may become more aware of the normal inconsistency of bead sizes within a package or hank. Pyramids will be lopsided if one bugle bead is longer than the other or if one end of a bugle bead is cut on an angle rather than perfectly straight. Accept the fact that further sorting is often required and make it a practice to do it. Otherwise, you'll find yourself pouting because you tried ignoring a crooked unit, only to admit ten minutes and ten inches later that you should have replaced the offending bead immediately.

Spacing

Evenly spaced motifs of course are the goal. For methods that consist of bead units, I generally use the length of my needle, or the length that my needle is able to travel, as my guide. As I begin to approach a corner, I like to preview my spacing needs by either measuring the last 12"-15" by eye or with a small ruler. If necessary, I start "fudging" the spacing, a little at a time, as I bead the rest of the units. This precaution is an easy way to achieve the appearance of equally spaced beads.

To eliminate the nuisance of removing beads when identical stitching is required, plan the bead spacing prior to stitching. It's easily accomplished by marking reference points in the binding with small silk straight pins and the aid of a ruler. Sometimes, it may even be necessary to bead several inches along the binding first, to provide accurate measurements, as it translates to the beads you are using. Avoid using marking tools that need to be removed with water. Remember, most beads don't like taking a bath.

Beginning and Ending a Thread

BEGINNING

Thread and knot the needle. Enter the binding from the wrong side, slipping the needle between the stitches that secure the binding to the backing. Exit at the point where the beading will begin, and give the needle a slight tug to pop the knot securely under the binding.

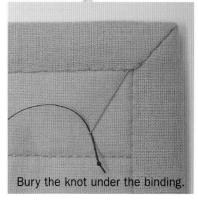

Bury the knot under the binding.

ENDING

There are two ways to end the thread, both the technique and the beads being featured will determine which one will work best. It's much easier to tie off if there is still ample thread to work with.

Pass the needle to the back side, exiting under the binding, just where the fold and backing meet. Complete the tie-off knot (see page 17) just under the edge of the binding. Travel the needle under the fold of the binding, and come out of the back of the binding about 1" away. Pull the thread through completely to secure the knot and tail under the binding. Clip the remaining thread end.

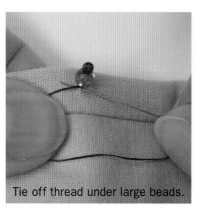

Tie off thread under the binding.

This method is a good choice when working with larger beads because it allows the knot to be easily hidden. To maintain proper thread tension, first take a tiny stitch just beneath the bead, and pull tightly. Now make a tie-off knot beneath the bead (see page 17). Reinsert the needle into the binding beneath the bead and travel about 1" away before coming back up to clip the thread end.

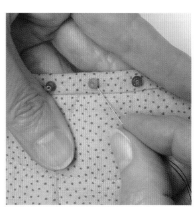

Tie off thread under large beads.

STITCHING

Hold the fabric somewhat taut in your hand to bead; using a frame isn't practical or necessary when beading bindings. A table or lapboard can help to support the weight of the quilt to avoid stretching and puckers. At times I utilize my left hand as a mini-hoop, my thumb and forefinger on top of the fabric and the remaining fingers below.

Stitching toward yourself vertically using the Basic Bead Backstitch, doesn't translate well when beading bindings. Instead, work horizontally. Begin on a corner with the quilt facing you. Always pull the thread completely through as each stitch is executed, maintaining an even tension. Generally, the direction you sew will be from right to left; for example, begin at the top-right corner of the quilt and stitch toward the top-left corner. If a specific beading sequence is necessary, a notation will be supplied in the instructions. Of course, feel free to tweak any of these methods to suit your comfort.

Finger placement can help support the binding during beading.

Bead "dots" can be positioned on the center top of the binding or along the outside folded edge. Either way, the results are fast and easy. The technique utilizes the Washer/Nut Method, where the "stopper bead" (Nut) holds the lower bead in place described on page 25. Larger beads, such as size 6° seeds or size 5° Triangles, are paired with seed beads, sizes 9°, 10°, or 11°. (The smaller bead must be larger than the hole of the lower bead.) Experiment using different bead colors, sizes, and spacing to achieve distinctly different effects. After the first unit is created, the needle travels—underneath—the binding, exiting where the second set is to be added, repeating as necessary.

With 1 large and 1 smaller bead threaded, hold the larger bead in place on the fabric and pass the needle back through its hole and into the fabric directly beneath the bead. Travel between the folds of the binding to the next bead location and repeat.

Good Morning

The center top of the binding is decorated with matte seed beads. The colors of the large size 6° and small size 11° were matched.

Be Lighthearted

Clear/Opaque white size 5° triangles are combined with size 10° black seed beads and placed along the outer edge of the binding.

Be Lighthearted

by Mary Stori, 2001, 33" x 35"
Photo by Sharon Risedorph

Sometimes just a small amount of beads are necessary to add details such as eyes, freckles, and buttons. These items add texture and don't conflict with the folk-art style of this quilt.

I've named this one Trio because 3 beads are attached with 1 stitch. This quick technique furnishes a simple, yet pleasing texture that is well suited to smaller size beads such as size 9°, 10°, and 11° seed beads when stitched to the binding's outside edge.

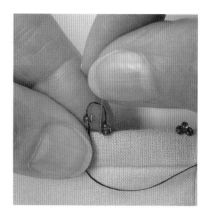

Pass the needle out at the edge of the binding add 3 seed beads. Enter the folded edge of the binding, about 1 bead width to the left of where you began. This shortened stitch will pop the middle bead up to sit above and between the other 2 beads. Travel underneath the binding, about the length of the needle, bringing it out through the fold. Repeat this sequence around the quilt.

Tropical Heartbeat #1

The high-contrast color of the matte fuchsia seed beads against the turquoise binding assures visibility, while the small bead size 11° guarantees a delicate outline.

Tropical Heartbeat #1

by Mary Stori, 2001, 15" x 15"

This quilt was designed to teach beading techniques on my Caribbean quilting cruise. The hearts display high energy beaded design motifs sewn with the Single-Bead Backstitch. The beaded "Trio" binding adds a splash of color for the finishing touch.

This edging is a long-time favorite with beaders because it's easily incorporated into many styles of beadwork and provides unity to a finished piece. Variations are fun to create by altering the sizes, numbers, and colors of the beads.

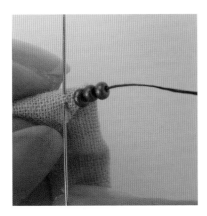

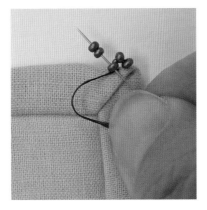

1. Beginning at the upper-right corner (stitching to the left), bring the needle out on the edge of the binding fold. String 3 seed beads, allowing them to drop to the binding in a line. Take a small stitch from front to back, near the top edge of the binding, about one-half a bead width from the where the 1st bead is sitting.

Note: This technique always starts with one 3 bead unit, followed by the addition of 2 bead units, from then on, to continue the pattern.

2. The 1st and 3rd bead should now sit next to each other, while the second straddles both. Next, pass the needle up through the hole of the third bead, taking care not to nick the fabric and string on 2 more beads, and pull the needle through all three beads.

3. Start again by taking a small stitch from front to back, about one-half bead width from where the 5th bead strung is now sitting, pulling the thread completely through as you did in step 1. The last bead strung should now sit next to the 3rd bead along the binding edge and the other bead (the 4th one) becomes the middle bead and will straddle the 3rd and 5th bead.

4. Repeat this sequence by always passing the needle back up through the last bead strung and adding 2 more beads around the perimeter of the binding.

Nature's Own
by Cindy Fitzpatrick, beaded by Mary.

The copper-beaded edging provides a handsome framework to complement the design of the quilt.

Civil War Stars
by Jan Vander Hill, beaded by Mary.

Consider using this texturized stitch to outline and add character to patchwork designs (see full quilt on page 11).

There are so many ways to use this version of the Lazy stitch, page 24. The placement, style, and color of bead will alter the design, yet the stitching manner remains consistent. Each unit is made of 3 beads; a large bead in the center, and a smaller one at each end. They are treated as 1 bead; therefore, it's important that the space allotted for the beads to lay on the binding be the same length as the bead unit. There have to be umpteen variations; the two examples shown are just to get you started.

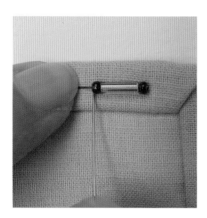

Bring the threaded needle out of the binding where you wish the beadwork to begin, either in the center or along the outside edge. Add 1 seed bead, 1 larger bead, and 1 seed bead. Let the beads drop onto the work, position them snugly in a line to the left of where you began, holding them in place with the tip of the needle. Pass the needle through the binding at the very end of the 3rd bead, and travel between the binding layers, exiting where the next "barbell" will begin. Repeat as you travel around the project.

Give Hugs

A lime-green twisted bugle bead and 2 seed beads make up the "barbell" units that are attached along the fold of the binding.

Heart to Heart

These barbells are placed in the center of the binding. Each unit features a triangle size 5° bead in the middle and a matching color seed bead on each side. Visual interest is increased by alternating the color scheme between blue and green.

If "eye-catching" is your goal, this nifty pattern will do the job. Use strings of beads, spaced diagonally along the binding, to add color and texture to your bindings. Each string can contain identically colored beads, or a secondary pattern can be created by using a number of different colors in each unit. The step-by-step process shown lends an asymmetrical appearance. Notice how the direction of the diagonal changes on each side of *Love of Many Colors*, pictured on the Table of Contents.

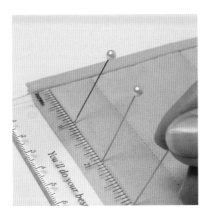

1. Begin in the upper-left seamline. Measure with a ruler and divide the length of the seam line into equal sections, aiming for about 1" spaces.

2. Mark the reference points with a straight pin, entering the seam line absolutely vertically to allow the tip of the pin to show on the back side. Reference pins can be placed one at a time or along the entire length.

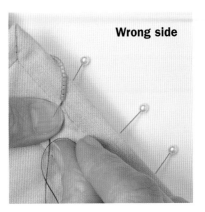

Wrong side

3. String enough seed beads, size 10° or smaller, to encase the thread completely when it is wrapped over the binding to the point where the straight pin is located. Now, working on the wrong side, pass the needle through the back binding, coming up in the front seamline at the first (1") pin. Add a sufficient number of seed beads and repeat.

Spacing adjustments may be required as the lower-left corner is reached. The last string must travel only over the front left side of the binding; do not carry the final string across the front of the binding at the corner.

This design mimics lace; refer to page 28 (Arch) for further information about this versatile stitch. The results vary greatly depending on the number and type of beads, the spacing, and even the location of the design. Here are two examples to explore.

Individual Units

Work the design in individual units as shown below, spacing the units as desired.

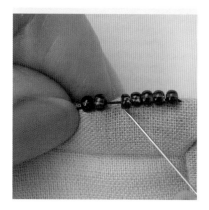

1. String 7 seed beads. Slide the last 2 beads slightly to the left. With the tip of the needle gently push the remaining 5 beads to the right, against the thread, and re-enter the binding (between where the 5th and 6th bead will sit). Avoid piercing the thread with the needle.

2. Travel through the binding layers, coming up where you want the next unit to begin. Pull snugly as each set of beads is stitched. Repeat, spacing the units as desired or as necessary to turn the corners.

Beading a Row

Use this variation to create a continuous row of beads.

Bring the threaded needle up through the binding's upper-right corner. String 9 bead seed beads, and slide them down the thread onto the fabric. Re-enter the binding between the 6th and 7th bead (avoid piercing the thread). Take a tiny stitch and bring the needle back up, almost in place. String another 9 beads and repeat in this manner completely around the quilt.

Love Note #2

The 7 blue seed-bead units sit along the edge of the binding in a series of individual motifs, providing an interesting texture.

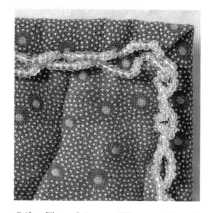

Like Touching a Warm Cloud

In this example, a second row of beads creates a fuller effect. After the first row is completed, bring the needle up within the body of the quilt (not the binding) a bead distance from the 1st row and across from the center of a unit in row 1. String 9 seed beads, beading the unit exactly as described for row 1. The ends of the units in row 1 should be in line with the center of the units in row 2; adjust spacing or number of beads in the units if necessary. Continue until row 2 is complete.

Create a zigzag look by sewing bugle bead and seed bead sets at opposing angles onto the top of the binding. As pictured, the finished binding width of ¼" was beaded using bugle beads, size 2°, combined with seed beads, size 11°. Leave about ⅜" of space between the seed beads along the outside edge of the binding and the seam line. (See *Meadow Flowers* on the title page.)

Meadow Flowers

The slight contrast of the bead colors helps to highlight the zigzag beading pattern.

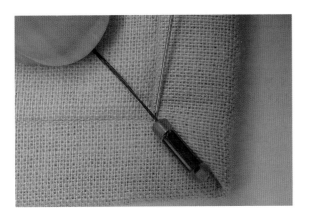

1. Bring the needle up through the outside lower-right corner miter. Thread 1 seed, 1 bugle, and 1 seed, and position this unit along the miter. Re-enter the miter at the very end of the last seed bead.

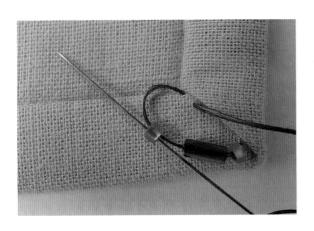

2. Take a stitch through the binding, back toward the bugle bead. Come up 1 seed bead width from where the needle entered (between the bugle and last seed bead). Pass the needle back through the the last seed bead in the direction it was originally strung.

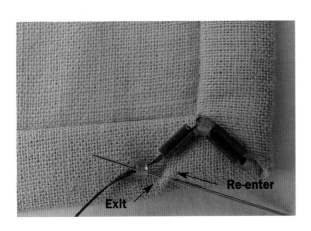

Re-enter

Exit

3. String 1 bugle and 1 seed bead. Position this unit at an angle (establishing the zigzag spacing you desire.) Re-enter the binding at the end of the seed bead and exit between the seed bead and bugle bead. Backstitch through the seed bead, and repeat.

PYRAMID

The triangular shape is formed with 3 seed beads and 2 bugle beads sewn as individual units. The look of this pattern will change dramatically as the size, color, and spacing of the beads are modified. Measuring is acceptable, but exact spacing isn't critical. If you eyeball the placement and fudge at the corners it will still look great! In the example shown the twisted bugle beads are size 3° and the seed beads are size 11°.

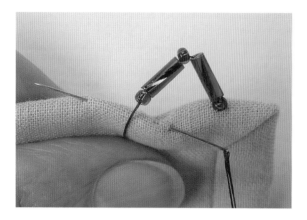

Starting at the upper-right corner, just left of the miter, bring the needle out on the fold of the binding. String on 1 seed bead, 1 bugle bead, 1 seed bead (this seed bead will be the "top" of the pyramid), 1 bugle bead, and 1 seed bead. Re-enter the fold of the binding about ¼" away and travel the needle along the inside of the fold, bringing it out at the fold about ¼" away. Repeat this sequence completely around the quilt.

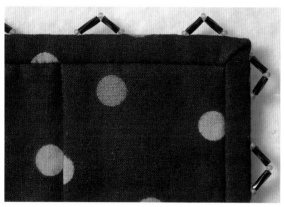

Love Note #3

The simple, two-color pyramid shapes repeat the color scheme of the quilt and punctuates the binding with sparkle.

NETTING

There are many different types of netting patterns; this example will help you understand the basics. Although it's the most time-consuming pattern offered in this chapter, the outcome is incredibly impressive. The first, or foundation row, is beaded using the pyramid technique; it is stitched consecutively to eliminate the spaces. A second row is joined onto the first, creating the netting. It's not difficult! The most challenging aspect will be to maintain proper thread tension. If it's too loose the beads will be floppy; if it's too tight you'll notice the netting will become wavy. Inconsistent sizes of bugle beads can effect how the beads sit together as the mesh grows. Re-sort your supply and use only uniform sizes. If your piece will be handled (not hung on a wall), consider using a double strand of the thinner Nymo, size B.

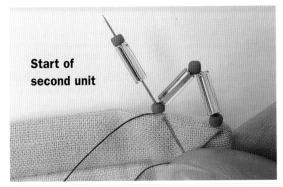

1. Starting in the upper right-corner, bring the needle out through the fold of the binding, almost on the miter. Thread on 1 seed bead, 1 bugle, 1 seed, 1 bugle, and 1 seed. Re-enter the fold of the binding about ¼" to the left, take a tiny stitch from front to back, and pass the needle back up and through the last seed bead. Start the second unit by adding 1 bugle, 1 seed, 1 bugle, and 1 seed. Again, take a tiny stitch. Repeat this beading order all the way around the quilt, tying off and beginning new thread as necessary.

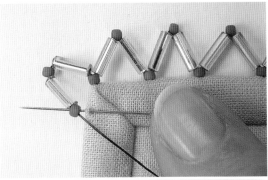

2. To turn the corner, be sure the seed bead of the last pyramid is placed as close to the top-left corner as possible. String the next unit as usual, but enter the binding around the corner, so the last seed bead in this unit sits close to the upper left side of the binding. The bottom "legs" of this pyramid will be much closer together, about ⅛" apart. Continue around the entire quilt. To end, pass through the first seed bead strung and tie off.

3. The Second Row: Begin again with a new thread at the upper-right corner of the binding. Pass the threaded needle through the 1st seed bead of the 1st row, the last bugle bead, and the last seed bead added. Pull the thread through completely.

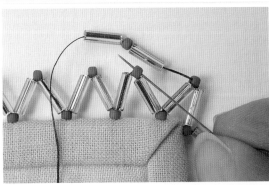

4. Thread on 1 bugle bead, 1 seed, 1 bugle bead. Working from right to left, pass the needle through the seed bead at the top of the 1st pyramid, pulling the thread firmly. Continue, always passing through the center seed bead of a pyramid in the 1st row before adding another unit. When new thread is required, pass the needle back through one "leg" (side) of a pyramid in the 1st row and tie off (see page 17). Start with a new thread and travel through a pyramid in row 1 up to where you stopped.

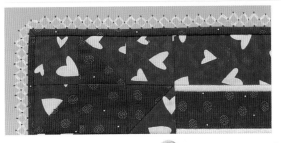

United We Stand

Clear bugle beads were used in combination with red and blue seed beads to create this intricate double-pyramid. (See photo of full quilt on page 15.)

This nifty design was developed to echo the embroidery motif I used to separate the blocks in my quilt, *Child's Play* (see page 22). The stitching order to create the X's developed quickly, yet the motifs overpowered the quilt when they were stitched close together, but looked ridiculous too far apart. After much trial and error, success was reached by adding Trio bead units between the bead X's. This pattern can be transformed by varying the color, style, size, and spacing of the beads. The motifs pictured in these examples were made using seed beads, size 11°, and twisted bugle beads, size 3°.

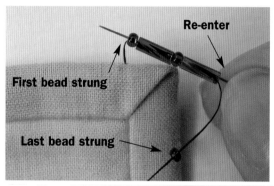

1. Bring the threaded needle out at the fold, about ¼" to the left of the upper-right corner. String 1 seed beed, 1 bugle , 1 seed, 1 bugle, and 1 seed bead. Re-enter the last bugle bead, bypassing the last seed bead, and travel back through the entire string. Be careful not to pierce the previous thread.

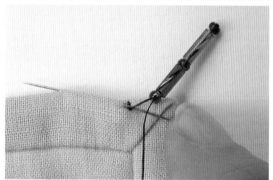

2. Insert the needle into the binding next to the original thread and travel to the left about ½", coming out at the fold. Pull the thread to tighten the beads.

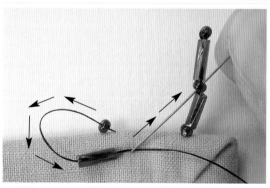

3. Add 1 seed bead and 1 bugle bead, and pass the needle through the center bead of the first leg, pulling the thread firmly. This creates the left bottom side of the X.

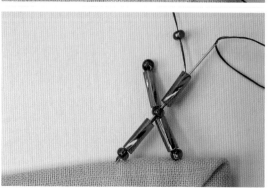

4. Now add 1 bugle bead and 1 seed bead. To secure the X, pass the needle through this second "leg" by re-entering the bugle (bypassing the last seed). Travel through to the binding, just under the bottom seed bead, pulling the thread snugly.

Travel the needle to the left about ¼", bead 1 Trio unit (see page 38 for instructions). Again, pass the needle through the binding about ¼" to the left. Bring the needle up at the fold and bead another "X" motif. Repeat sequence completely around the quilt; maintain constant tension and adjust spacing as needed.

If texture, or a sense of growth and energy, would benefit your quilt, try this pattern. It works best using seed beads, size 11°, but larger beads could be substituted. (See *Love Note #4*, Acknowledgments page.)

1. Begin in the lower-right corner with the edge of the binding close to you, sewing from right to left. Bring the needle out of the binding at the very edge of the fold, at the right side corner. String 12 seed beads, position them tightly in a line along the edge of the binding. Enter the binding at the very end of the last bead (the 12th one strung), take a tiny ¹/₁₆" stitch to the left. Pull the thread through completely.

2. Thread on 9 seed beads to create a string of beads. Pass the needle back through the 4th bead from the bottom in the string.

New seed bead →

3. Add 1 seed bead and re-enter the 2nd bead strung, traveling up through the 1st bead. Pull taut.

Love Note #4

4. Pull the thread gently, just to eliminate the gaps. Enter the binding near the thread and take a tiny ¹/₁₆" stitch to the left, exiting at the fold of the binding.

Repeat the pattern by adding a line of 12 beads, followed by another 9 bead unit. Continue around the quilt, adjusting spacing as needed by reducing the number of beads in the 12 bead units at the corners.

RESOURCES

NEEDLES & SCISSORS

Jean S. Lyle
P. O. Box 289
Quincy, IL 62306
Telephone: 217-222-8910
Email: jslyle@adamas.net
Website: www.jslyle.com

HAND-DYED FABRICS AND BUTTONS

Primrose Gradations
P.O. Box 6
Two Harbors, MN 55616
Telephone: 888-393-2787
Website: www.dyearts.com

BEADS

TWE/BEADS
PO Box 55
Hamburg, NJ 07419
Telephone: 973-209-1517
Fax: 973-209-4471
Email: info@twebeads.com
Website: www.twebeads.com

Fire Mountain Gems
One Fire Mountain Way
Grants Pass, OR 97526
Telephone: 800-423-2319
Fax: 800-292-3473
Email: firemtn@cdsnet.net
Website:
www.firemountaingems.com

SEWING MACHINES

Pfaff American Sales
610 Winters Avenue
P.O. Box 566
Paramus, NJ 07653
Telephone: 201-262-7211

BATTING

Hobbs Bonded Fibers
P.O. Box 2521
Waco, TX 76710
Telephone: 254-741-0040
Fax: 254-772-7238

MEET THE AUTHOR

Mary began teaching herself to quilt while recovering from back surgery in the mid-1980s. She had planned to return to her career of cooking-school owner, instructor, and cookbook author, but after discovering the world of quilting, beading, and wearable art, her energies were redirected.

She is a lecturer, teacher, author, fashion judge, and quilter whose award-winning work has appeared in national and international shows. She's appeared on HGTV's "Simply Quilts" and "Sew Perfect", and an episode of Fons & Porter's PBS show "Love of Quilting" featured Mary's quilts. Her one-of-a-kind garments have traveled with the 1992, 1994, 1997, and 1998 Fairfield Fashion Shows.

Mary's writing credits are extensive. She's written articles or been featured in scores of quilt magazines and publications! This is her fourth quilt-related book. In addition, Mary wrote, The Stori of Beaded Embellishment, published by Martingale & Company, 2001, and The Wholecloth Garment Stori (1998), and The Stori Book of Embellishing (1994), both published by American Quilter's Society. Inspiration guaranteed!

Her work is often humorous, and frequently features fun embellishments and fine hand quilting. She designed The Mary Stori Collection for Kona Bay Fabrics and her own line of trapunto quilting stencils for Quilting Creations. Traveling worldwide as a quilt tour host for Specialty Tours and to present lectures, workshops, and fashions shows keeps her motivated!

For workshop and lecture information, contact:

Mary Stori, W 811 Taylor Trail, Brodhead, WI 53520, Email: dstori@earthlink.net, Website: www.quilt.com/MaryS